Pray Tell
in the
Key of Blue

Pray Tell
in the
Key of Blue

Terry Minchow-Proffitt

Clare Songbirds
Publishing House

Clare Songbirds Publishing House Poetry Series
ISBN 978-1-957221-18-2

Clare Songbirds Publishing House
Pray Tell in the Key of Blue © 2024 Terry Minchow-Proffitt

Printed in the United States of America
FIRST EDITION

All quotations of Scripture are from
The Five Books of Moses: Genesis, Exodus, Leviticus, Numbers, Deuteronomy
translated by Everett Fox.

140 Cottage Street
Auburn, New York 13021
www.claresongbirdspub.com

For

Mat and Cathy Hartig
with glad love and gratitude.

ACKNOWLEDGMENTS

What goes without saying can't be said enough. I am immeasurably grateful to John Burns, Belden Lane, Matthew Lippman, Daye Phillippo, and Guy Sayles for their willingness to anoint this chapbook with their wise and honest light; to my daughter, Hannah, whose beautiful presence and art have accompanied all my poems; and to the gifted editors at Clare Songbirds Publishing House. With you by my side, we helped Lucky find his footing in the wide blue world.

Sandy, Zak, and Hannah, I am most at home with God, my haven and heart, with and through you.

Contents

~Preface~

This book is dedicated to my dear friends Mat and Cathy Hartig. Throughout our friendship, their love shared a deep longing to build a dream home together. I cannot begin to name the number of properties they visited or describe the various possible floor plans we discussed with such energy and detail over dinner. Only this one constant: The home, Cathy insisted, must have a room with a window that faced west. She wanted one day to sit and share the sunset over wine and cheese with family and friends, especially Mat.

Then Myelodysplastic Syndrome barged uninvited into Cathy's life. Amidst the increasing prospect of diminishing health, the grind of one more treatment, and the travail of recurrent stays in the hospital, she and Mat pressed on with their dream. This proved to be more than consoling. They happened upon the perfect fixer-upper, a neglected place with "good bones" warranting more of a rebuild than a remodel. Throughout their measured days, nothing stopped Cathy and Mat. They endured and prevailed in a way that would have made William Faulkner proud. They moved in time for Cathy to savor their new home. By then, however, she was full of heart but too frail to make it up to the quirky third-floor room with the west window (a perfect place for a nook one day, she said). Still, I trust that in her mind's eye, surrounded by all her beloved, Cathy toasted the sunset and christened their new home with wine and cheese. On the upcoming Christmas Eve of 2018, Cathy was taken from us by a rare disease I still cannot pronounce or spell on my own, much less understand why this could happen to someone with such a future in her eyes. Cathy's adventurous spirit defied whatever tried to clip her wings. She had all the vital goods: energy, resolve, honesty. And the sturdy stuff of a well-tempered faith, hope, and love always remained. It's enough to make you blue.

A while later, with the gale of grief still howling, Mat and I were hunkered over our Captain and Diet Cokes at a local pub. Much of the conversation was about how he was, rattling around alone in their house without his Cathy. All this even though she was still in his heart. After a bit, when hard was hard enough, I said, "You do know that Cathy deeded me the third floor of your house, right? She always said it would be a perfect place for a poet to do what poets do." He laughed, then said, "When do you wanna start?" Later, after a parking lot hug, I turned for my truck. Mat called out, "Hang on! He reached into his pocket, worked a key off his keyring, and handed it to me. "Come and go anytime. This was Cathy's housekey." There, in my palm, was her key. Her key was blue.

Pray Tell in the Key of Blue was written from the west window on the third floor of Mat and Cathy's dream home. Without this room, this window, Cathy and Mat's loving resolve and generosity, no little book of poetry in your hand. The blue key sang out to me: of blues, of the opening of our moans, of a color and a sound, an entrance, a way in. I was led to the first creation narrative in the Book of Genesis; then, as a surprise, Lucky came knocking with the twists and turns of his life. Lucky's challenges do not reflect Mat and Cathy's lives in any particular way, but they aspire to be about all our lives together in every way. We can all be as blue and faithful as Lucky. The Lord of Life, every day, is hard at work sharing our load, singing our blues, and wrangling some semblance of order from the havoc of our lives. At least, that's what Cathy taught me: Sunsets tend toward solitude, but they are meant to be shared.

Terry Minchow-Proffitt

First Day

At the beginning of God's creating
of the heavens and the earth,
when the earth was wild and waste,
darkness over the face of Ocean,
rushing-spirit of God hovering over the face of the waters—

God said: Let there be light! And there was light.
God saw the light: that it was good.
God separated the light from the darkness.
God called the light: Day! And the darkness he called: Night!
There was setting, there was dawning: one day.

I

Light galore falls from blue sky,
angles over the shadowed gut
of an eroded ravine where Lucky stumbles
upon the flipped ATV two days too late.
He can hardly make out the boy's still body
stuck in the sepulchral mud and shallow flow
of yesterday's rain. *That's Early's boy, Joaquin.*

Lucky breathes in
what morning light misses,
how it slants into the riprapped gully
from the east, ignites
the tumped-over red Suzuki 250
but slights the boy's body
pinned in the dark below.

The Lord closes in,
hovers over this havoc.
Borne on great wings
pinioned solely by the fierce
spread and sweep
of unbearable yearning:
Let there be light!

II

It's all over town about the search for the missing boy.
Lucky backs away, dials 911, says what he sees
from where he's at in these woods he walks
when life's too much. He lowers
his back against a cottonwood to stare
down the blue distance: a ways away, a speck
of neon-orange flashes from the sedge.

It's Joaquin's cap, flung and rearin' up.
Everything in Lucky balks:
Lord, this here's hard to swaller.
Ever boy oughta git to play, Lord.
You might jimmy Day from Night,
but that don't keep the thief from calling
with a punch to the gut.

Is that you, Lord? A thief in the night?
Or is that ole Scratch? Or Lady Luck?
All's I know is I'm 'fraid
my light's 'bout out.
A mild breeze stirs Lucky's prayer
into the cool clatter
of shade above.

III

Let's call it a day. The Lord spits,
humbled and hurt and apt
to feel there's never enough
time at the speed of light
to quell the havoc. The Lord broods:
I thought my light would suffice,
be the first and final word. Mulls and mulls

the likes of Joaquin's crushed radiance
in all that mud, the very cerulean hit
Lucky's heart must now
take in. The Lord's always been given
to the occasional
distant gaze,
especially as night turns

on Day One. Having seen what lies
at the bottom of the primordial ruckus,
all the drowned bodies, sunken hulks,
and lost treasures, the Lord laments,
longs for a different dark, prays a prayer prayed
by all the tired spirits who welcome sleep
on the tail end of a long day: *My yoke is light.*

Second Day

God said:
Let there be a dome amid the waters,
and let it separate waters from waters!
God made the dome
and separated the waters that were below the dome
from the waters that were above the dome.
It was so.
God called the dome: Heaven!
There was setting, there was dawning: second day.

I

Imagine a longing
like the one Joaquin
never had enough time
to put his back into, one that bleeds
through blue, like the vow
Lucky and the Lord made
to learn to live together

in this world. Here. Where blue
sound and color sigh with the broken
light of love.
Because there is no away, no distance
in the Lord, there is a way.
It's how the Lord yearns to swoop
in all wings and snatch by the throat

the dark pit of ever-crumbling ravines,
how light rivets the indigo night
porous with stars as far as the eye
can't see, inexhaustibly dreambanged
by love's combustible outrage into a *firmament,*
the Good Book's word for how vaulted awe
bobs and blazes star upon star to the heavens.

II

Lucky's off-kilter and missing turns
on his walk back. He knows well the twiney
way home, yet he cannot unsee Joaquin's body
and what it tells of a long night
before any semblance of mottled light makes landfall,
how the waters of chaos went on a tear
to steal from Joaquin what he's just begun to love.

Lucky feels parched,
doused in the sweat
of an old longing.
The part of him that is bad to drink
sidles up and begins to entertain
how he might drop by Red's
and take a load off.

Rain's gonna fall.
Water, water, everywhere water
will not let up. Cloudburst, its blue outcry
absorbed, divvied up
by the Lord's firmament
to riddle the land brunt with thirst.
Y'all staying dry?

III

Red's Lounge, where Lucky's
become a regular of late on live music night,
seems too small when the hour is late,
a tiny coracle cast adrift in the middle
of evening. Still, the Lord has a sure eye
on the ardent glare and swagger of sweat-lit ecstasies
whorling yellow from the raised windows.

Cash Only. Such beseeching.
Lucky's had a few
too many. He can't see
past his eyes right now:
Joaquin's crushed body;
Ruby's full figure, hot and coming on.
All these fallen bodies

Lucky cannot resist. The whelming lament
and lust pour through Ruby and Lucky
in the back parking lot. Done.
He hikes up his pants; she pats down her blue dress.
He dawdles his sorry ass home to his wife and kids.
Day breaks overhead, a fading
dome of beaucoup stars.

Third Day

God said:
Let the waters under the heavens be gathered to one place,
and let the dry land be seen!
It was so.
God called the dry land: Earth! And the gathering of the waters
he called: Seas!
God saw that it was good.
God said:
Let the earth sprout forth with sprouting growth,
plants that seed forth seeds, fruit trees that yield fruit,
after their kind, (and) in which is their seed, upon the earth!
It was so.
The earth brought forth sprouting growth,
plants that seed forth seeds, after their kind,
trees that yield fruit, in which is their seed, after their kind.
God saw that it was good.
There was setting, there was dawning: third day.

I

On the Third Day, the Lord reckons
undivided light and ocean alone are not enough
to buck back chaos: light must
make landfall, turn earthen,
carry a telluric flame
for radiant dust, vow: I live
longing to long, for want of you.

Summoned from beneath
the heaving seas, land wrests itself,
rises with enough crust to sprout: a shambling
welter of living stones, fox tail, and blue desert sage.
Limbs bend anointed with sweet
peachlove and plumjoy. The Lord raises
his face on the Third Day: *Good!*

Earth itches to ramble and conceive.
Seeds pine for falling.
When there are people, blood will boil to sycamore and tendril.
When there are horses, the apple's core will ride far.
Rooks and jays will one day sow riot days on end.
For now, on the Third Day, only the Lord's breath
to spread the tumbleweed diaspora for miles.

II

Heaven knows what the day might bring
while Lucky sits on the side of the bed
holding his head in his hands.
Effie and the kids have gone
to church. He'd like to keep lying
hungover in bed, but his thirst
and his head won't allow it.

Beyond Lucky's open window, a breeze
riffles the bedroom curtains. The crepe myrtle bottle tree
sways just enough to whisper his way
from beyond the garden plot.
Lucky's sure of what's coming. He could bolt
before the kids return in their church clothes
to take him at his word, corner him with their eyes.

The lucent curtains' sway, the bottle tree's
bluebrooding over the fallow garden,
the smell of Effie's pot roast in the oven—
all this native tenderness Lucky calls home
unraveling in the frothy dark with Ruby behind Red's.
Are you feeling better, Daddy?
See, I drew Jesus on a donkey for you.

III

What are the odds
of our rampant green world traipsing to
from seacrush, a melee of veined leaves
and gangly roots riding out
the wind and the rain
once the Lord exalts dumb dust
with the quiet, diurnal doting of lightfall?

Not great, I'd guess.
So much death and distance defied
by the Lord's tender spot
for the cellular urgency
of how the blue beyond
might spurn the speed of light
and take to the amble and sprawl

of earthbound life. There the likes of
the twisted-trunked Tamarisk flounces
forth blue-green from the blue-mountain desert. Feathers out
in wild thirst and foliage through the wavering
heat and drought dust, the vexed heart
yet to rise rife. Odds are, every day's
the Third Day somewhere.

Fourth Day

God said:
Let there be lights in the dome of the heavens
to separate the day from the night,
that they may be for signs—for set-times, for days and years,
and let them be for lights in the dome of the heavens,
to provide light upon the earth!
It was so.
God made the two great lights,
the greater light for ruling the day
and the smaller light for ruling the night,
and the stars.
God placed them in the dome of the heavens
to provide light upon the earth,
to rule the day and the night,
to separate the light from the darkness.
God saw that it was good.
There was setting, there was dawning: fourth day.

I

Neither Ruby nor doubles of Four Roses
can help Lucky get shut of what he can't unsee:
the boy's still there, a vision of a little heap
of crushed flesh in late spring.
A blue fire behind Lucky's eyes
licks like blind greed
right through the kindling

racked in his chest, leaves him
charred,
his very soul bellies up
barren:
I'm dry. Yellow Label's good,
he says to Red, *Hit me again.*
Lucky can't lick his hankering

throat. Knows to shove off but settles in:
Keep 'em coming. Once more
smudges out one more
memory he can't manage
yet won't let lie: his neighbor's son's body
still enough to be missed in broad daylight.
What was his name again? Lucky mumbles.

II

I need some light, more or less,
the Lord says, squinting. *It's getting hard*
to see what I'm up to by my own eyes.
So, beneath the stars, Sun and Moon hop to,
the greater and the lesser lights, light that lands.
That's good. Light like this
buys me time.

The Lord's more than a tad giddy, having never had time
when creation had no light of its own.
So, this is "viz-uh-bull"? The Lord tries out
these three syllables for what our light can do.
Intimate as the tide's pull, staggering
as a malefic blast of noonday heat
to the face in August, Moon and Sun

phase into play their daily alloy of mutation, collision,
and plummet, the profligate seed and mulch
of due seasons, hefty leaf-fall of now and no more.
Days spin into nights, a splurge
of blue whirl older than history.
The Lord now kneels and sees
long before we have eyes and knees.

III

Lord, we can't help but point out that
Lucky's noticed of late how quiet you've grown
since the Third Day. Are you wistful
for that banner First Day, burdened
by the spectacle of unseen light?
See, life by our light bends to the iris,
jangles the nerves if you're lucky

to be alive. Seeing, like ours, can be too much.
How it levels things between us: the what's-what
of angle and jut in time, like when we behold
no love without loss, or how a mother's dead child looms.
At the mercy of this life, we're made to mourn
the grim ambit of what we can't get but must get used to—the real gaps
where we fall into our dismal trifling.

Matter of fact, go ahead, brood some more, Lord.
Whelp and wince at all the settings and dawnings
we must hold, marvel at how we bear up blue
at the mercy of our greater-and lesser-lit lives.
We'll press on with you at a dim distance.
Wait, is that a limp? You'll come around.
We know you've got it in you to see us through.

Fifth Day

God said:
Let the waters swarm of living beings, and let fowl
fly above the earth, across the dome of the heavens!
God created the great sea-serpents
and all living beings that crawl about, with which the waters
swarmed, after their kind,
and all winged fowl after their kind.
God saw that it was good.
And God blessed them, saying:
Bear fruit and be many and fill the waters in the seas,
and let the fowl be many on earth!
There was setting, there was dawning: fifth day.

I

Thank God it's Friday, the Lord says, *Let it swarm!*
Light created and beyond yonder uncreated,
who knows which is which? If you can,
measure the mercy of blue marlins and purple martins,
scale-shimmer and feather-flutter,
stab of spear-snout and wing-tuck
soar the blue bodies of ocean and air.

They swarm with swarms,
nervy and blessed, fervid creatures
of enfolding airs and waters
that cannot be teased apart, all in
cahoots, marlin breathes what it swims,
martin breathes what it soars.
Swarms swarm our blue planet.

Sure, from a distance, say,
a moon's eye view, we see blue,
blue marble blue. But closer up and in?
Hazier, most days, a hazard to regard,
but . . . yes, there too. We make do
by a slew of blue. Sweet Spirit blue.
It's all we breathe; how we swarm.

II

Let's say, you're walking north up King
one Friday afternoon and hang a left on Spring.
You're liable to see a small man bent over, hoeing
a garden patch behind a blue house beside a blue bottle tree.
For no reason, he will stop hoeing and look up
as you pass. You'll look away and keep walking.
You won't know it, but that'd be Lucky.

Lucky knows Ruby'll be waiting for him tonight
at Red's. He knows this heat has lit into him
as he hoes his garden earth. His wife,
Effie, knows something's up
if not all. Lucky stops weeding
and looks up, leaning on his hoe.
Where he's at, prays, *Good Lord,*

Lord of the birds and the fishes, Lord of this spring
day calling, Lord of all this that's swarming
me and my sap, help me to do what's right
and stay away from Red's and Ruby tonight.
Help me go back inside to my own.
Lucky drops the hoe and goes in to grab a drink
with cupped hands from the kitchen sink.

III

Lucky turns off the faucet
and wipes his mouth with his hand.
Stares out the window above the sink,
rapt before a great and wide nothing.
Something in the blue
calls him, *Let's get some air, Lucky.*
Come away with me. He can't help but.

Lucky steps out like he's lost
to an empty porch swing. Eases down and sways.
Lord, where's my thirst? He's startled
to be as quiet and still and unfamiliar
as he's been in a month of Sundays.
There's plenty more weeding to be done
but here is where Lucky stays put.

Lucky would later allow, right then and there
over the sink, how he was laid to heart:
It was the strangist thang. *The Lord of a sudden*
musta stole into the lower holler of my chest
and swallered my foolish hankering whole.
That's how Lucky held to being
quenched and full in this here world.

Sixth Day

God said:
Let the earth bring forth living beings after their kind,
herd-animals, crawling things, and the wildlife of the earth after
their kind!
It was so.
God made the wildlife of the earth after their kind,
and the herd-animals
after their kind, and all crawling things of the soil after their kind.
God saw that it was good.

God said:
Let us make humankind, in our image, according to our likeness!
Let them have dominion over the fish of the sea, the fowl of the
heavens, animals, all the earth, and all crawling things that crawl
about upon the earth!
God created humankind in his image,
in the image of God did he create it,
male and female did he create them.
God blessed them,
God said to them:
Bear fruit and be many and fill the earth
and subdue it!

God said:
Here, I give you
all plants that bear seeds that are upon the face of all the earth,
and all trees in which there is tree fruit that bears seeds,
for you shall they be, for eating;
and also for all the living things of the earth, for all the fowl
of the heavens, for all that crawls about upon the earth in which
there is living being—
all green plants for eating.
It was so.
Now God saw all that he had made,
and here: it was exceedingly good!
There was setting, there was dawning: the sixth day.

I

It's like I used to be, walking the fields, Lucky thinks,
still swaying full-hearted in the porch swing while imagining
the feel of furrows, fencelines, and woods he once hunted
as a boy. Hunted out even then, their hush held
no bear, deer, or bobcat to speak of
but enough rabbit, squirrel, quail
and Ghost Dog rumors to declare he was

a hunter. But he rarely fired his dad's .22.
He was shy even then, the spell
of absence eating at him. All he wanted
was to disappear enough to slip up
close on what wild was left, that there
secret skittering near at hand, the flushed
whirr of a bobwhite's sudden flight

from the brush. With time, the boy came into his own,
exiled by Four Roses, left with nothing but
one day to the next and enough empty
to fill Lucky blue with lack.
He could not deny these days without give,
all what ate at him over the sink before the good Lord
waded in and took aholt of his thirst.

II

In time a train at the distant crossing
blows its warning and brings Lucky back:
locomotive racket,
the trundling on
of fully freighted cars
with graffitied steel
containers of passing promises.

Lucky checks his watch, can't believe the time.
He gets up, stands on the porch, stretches,
and looks up to the corner of King and Spring.
The school bus'll be here drekly,
he thinks. *Effie will too.*
She'll be as surprised as Lucky is glad
when he shows up for once in a blue moon

to meet the kids
as they step off the bus so small
and all smiles. Lucky's all prayer:
Pray tell, Lord, who was I to skirt this?
Is it too late for me to pick them back up
and carry my own in this life as it comes?
Suffer the little children . . .

III

The Lord moves heaven and earth
for the Judas Tree to flower
mauve-pink each spring
before giving way
to heart-shape green
leaves after three weeks.
A small tree with a short life.

Quick, think of joy!
How long is it? How tall or deep?
How much does it weigh?
Is joy's hue blue?
How many lives
does it save?
Who can say?

Only the Lord knows how light
must land to be light, must
find its level like water upon the earth,
be borne by flushed bobwhites, brief
bursts of Redbuds, and bent backs hoeing
good earth between dawning and setting,
the coming in and going out.

Seventh Day

Thus were finished the heavens and the earth,
with all of their array.
God had finished, on the seventh day
his work that he had made,
and then he ceased, on the seventh day,
from all his work that he had made.
God gave the seventh day his blessing,
and he hallowed it, for on it he ceased from all his work,
that by creating, God had made.
These are the begettings of the heavens and the earth.

I

Lucky wakes early Easter Sunday.
He lies there, still suspect of a good night's sleep
and rising without a drink. He pulls
his church shoes out of the closet.
They're still covered in dust
from what happened when he was
beyond blue behind Red's

the last time he duded up.
Lucky grabs out a rag, the Kiwi polish,
and spiffs his brogues to a raven shine.
Dust lifts in the light. He takes in hand
his first cup of Maxwell House
to rouse the kids for Sunday
comics over Captain Crunch.

Effie rises. *There's my Easter*,
Lucky thinks. Quiet and a mite
nervous about her new Lucky,
Effie prays he stays put this time
when flat-out thirst comes calling.
It'll sure as hell come, she knows,
but thirsty Jesus rose, so Lucky can too.

II

Besides, the Lord never quits forgivin',
so I reckon I'll try again, Effie thinks,
Seven times seventy. With all this,
they walk to King's Temple
in their Easter best. They see others
doing the same on this spring
day, the surety of greening lawns

and blue-blue sky.
How many Easters, Lord? Effie wonders.
She reckons she's missed nary a one.
The good Lord must know I need the practice.
Effie smiles and grabs Lucky's hand,
her eyes straight ahead on the kids.
Lucky locks his fingers in Effie's for nerve.

Prays, *Back, Beast! Back in yore hole.*
I don't want no part of you.
In the distance, the perfect pitch of praise
rises with the day as they draw closer, a joy
startled and chased by song. They quicken
to join these voices where lost chances
leap into chorus.

III

There's a porch where the Good Lord lounges,
drinks in all these begettings of heaven and earth:
Don't have a duck, Lucky. A little rest would do us all good.
Remember when you wished for a glass eye
or one arm, some excuse sad enough for you to fall
into Ruby's arms and that bottle without a bottom?
Come unto me. Take a load off. Hear that mourning dove?

Sure, even now, there's more
the Lord could work on and answer for,
but that can wait, like Effie's Monday at Dollar General
and Lucky's search in earnest for something steady.
Yes, it's all too much. So the Lord shushes
all future fret and such to savor the uneven finish
of forever and now, how creation yet shines again

in janky time and space and heart,
how a prayer like Lucky's can rise from King Street
on knees bent blue, *I'll drink*
from this here cup you offer, this hand
I hold, this hold you have on me and mine.
I'm countin' on you to wade in deep and
drink me down, Lord, before I drown.

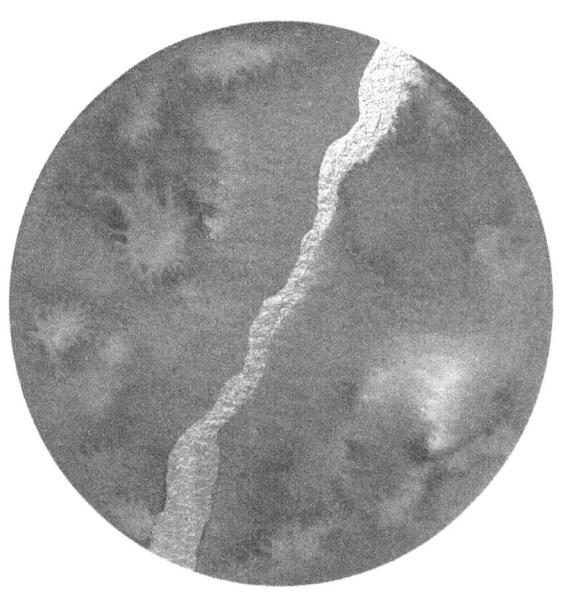

Terry Minchow-Proffitt lives in St. Louis, Missouri. He was raised in the rural Delta of eastern Arkansas and draws great inspiration from this region and its people. As a retired pastor, he now doubles down on reading and writing, savoring the silence and stillness that make this luxury possible. His daughter claims, "He buys books like he's immortal."

His poems have appeared in various journals and magazines. *Pray Tell: Poems in the Key of Blue* is his fourth collection of poems. His previous books are *Seven Last Words* (2015), *Chickentrain: Poems from the Arkansas Delta* (2016), and *Sweetiebetter* (2019).

www.ingramcontent.com/pod-product-compliance
Lightning Source LLC
Chambersburg PA
CBHW051600120626
46551CB00013B/1610